BUSES IN
ALL-OVER ADVERTS

RICHARD WALTER

AMBERLEY

Front Cover: Films come and go very quickly throughout the year but their pre-publicity advertising can be seen everywhere from TV, magazines, bus shelters and buses. Arriva London North Wrightbus-bodied New Routemaster LT173 (LTZ 1173), pictured on Waterloo Bridge, was one of a few NRMs to promote *Mama Mia – Here We Go Again*. The images from the film publicity fitted the bus sides well.

Rear Cover: During 2019, Lothian Buses prepared Wrightbus Gemini 3-bodied hybrid Volvo B5TL 584 (SJ67 MGV) in striking colours for Pride Edinburgh. It is seen at Newhaven en route to Edinburgh Airport.

First published 2019

Amberley Publishing
The Hill, Stroud
Gloucestershire, GL5 4EP

www.amberley-books.com

Copyright © Richard Walter, 2019

The right of Richard Walter to be identified as the Author of this work has been asserted in accordance with the Copyright, Designs and Patents Act 1988.

ISBN 978 1 4456 9191 6 (print)
ISBN 978 1 4456 9192 3 (ebook)

British Library Cataloguing in Publication Data.
A catalogue record for this book is available from the British Library.

Origination by Amberley Publishing.
Printed in the UK.

Introduction

I suspect that there is a divide of opinion on the use of all-over advertising on buses. Some see it as an unsightly distortion of the appearance of the vehicle, covering, in many cases, an appealing and attractive fleet livery. Others, like myself, find the whole concept interesting and an opportunity to photograph something just a little different.

Advertising on buses goes back a long way. It started in the days of the horse-drawn bus, when side painted boards and posters were widely used. Both local and national businesses saw the potential of having their product or services seen every day across not only busy towns and cities but rural areas too. The bus companies recognised an easy means of income generation. In time, adverts became much more colourful, ambitious and prominent. By the seventies the trend had set in for part or the whole of a bus to be hand-painted with elaborate designs. Since then, the all-over advert has evolved over the years with wrap-round vinyls now being widely used. Whereas in the past a bus had to be taken out of service to prepare it and apply the advertising, and again at the end of the contract to repaint it back into fleet livery, the application and removal of vinyls is quick and easy. There are complete wraps, contravision (which often restricts the views of passengers as it might cover the windows too), mega rear adverts and extended side ones.

For this book I have gathered together a selection of photographs, which I hope show a good representation of some of the multitude of campaigns that have appeared over the years. Many of the pictures are from Edinburgh, where I grew up, and demonstrate the changes over the years in not only the complexity of designs, but also the types of buses that have adorned advertising messages. There are photographs from London, which is probably the place you will find the most all-over adverts. When London took delivery of a thousand New Routemasters with their controversial style and clear glazed staircases, the opportunity arose for advertisers to make use of the buses for short term all-over vinyl wraps and I have included a number of examples of the wide range of products, fashion, films, musicals and holiday destinations that have appeared. There are also photographs from across the rest of the country, including Belfast and Dublin, where Coca-Cola and Heinz baked beans and tomato ketchup were particularly well promoted.

Be prepared for a sea of vivid colours, gasp at some of the most outrageous ads, puzzle over what some of the campaigns are actually for and hopefully experience some nostalgia for ones you remember from days gone by.

My thanks go to Andrew Chalmers, Murdoch Currie, Mark Lyons, Donald MacRae, Thomas McReynolds, Gordon Scott and Alistair Train for their photographic contributions and assistance. All are credited for their particular work. The uncredited pictures were taken by myself.

When buses were hand-painted, drawings were used to assist the craftsmen applying the designs. This photo shows the template for an advert for Wylies, Ford car dealers.

Eastern Scottish Alexander RV-bodied Volvo Ailsa B55-10 VV78 (HSF 78X) is seen with the final Wylies artwork applied in the old Edinburgh bus station. Many campaigns had to be painted on vehicles with different body styles, therefore designs had to be adaptable to ensure the basic advert looked the same.

The Appleyard car dealership in Edinburgh had three different all-over adverts running at the same time. The eye-catching Jaguar design appeared on Lothian Region Transport Alexander-bodied Leyland Atlantean PDR1A/1 353 (SSF 353H), which was amongst the last of its batch to be withdrawn. It is seen at the Granton end of service 17.

Buses and booze. In the early days of advertising, beer was a popular subject to promote. Lothian Region Transport Alexander-bodied Leyland Atlantean PDR1/1 898 (JSC 898E) is seen in the first of two all-over adverts it carried for Diamond Export. The photo was taken at Eastfield, Edinburgh.

Lothian Region Transport Alexander-bodied Leyland Atlantean AN68/1R 636 (GSC 636X), in a bright and attractive livery for Wimpey Homes, approaching the Greenbank terminus in Edinburgh. The bus was later enhanced with two cat eyes on either side of the destination box.

The Loch Ness Monster made an appearance on the side of Lothian Region Transport Alexander-bodied Leyland Atlantean AN68/1R 542 (SSG 542R), which promoted the Scottish Experience Visitor Centre in Edinburgh. It is seen here leaving Waverley Bridge.

By far the longest running advertising contract in Edinburgh (1985–95) was on Lothian Region Transport Alexander-bodied Leyland Atlantean AN68/1R 658 (GSC 658X), for the *Daily Record* and *Sunday Mail* Scottish newspapers. It was later to receive a fleet coloured front. Along with other companies, Lothian decided passengers could be confused if a bus approached with a different-coloured front, so many of the later advertisements did not have an all-over effect.

Whilst not a common practice, some advertisers wished illustrations on the bus roof to attract people looking down from bridges, offices and shops. Lothian Region Transport ECW-bodied Leyland Olympian 710 (A710 YFS) carried its Wimpy restaurants design on top as well as on the sides. It is captured from above passing Waverley Bridge, Edinburgh.

A particularly intricate all-over ad for Terry's Harlequin chocolates appeared on Lothian Region Transport ECW-bodied Leyland Olympian ONTZ11/2R 669 (OFS 669Y), seen heading up Lothian Road, Edinburgh.

Lothian Region Transport ECW-bodied Leyland Olympian ONTZ11/2R 736 (A736 YFS) entered service as new in this advertising livery for Wm McEwan's 80 Shilling ale. McEwan was one of a number of breweries associated with bus adverts for many years. The bus is seen passing through Bristo Square in Edinburgh.

Also new into service with an all-over ad and seen passing Greyfriars Bobby in Edinburgh was Lothian Region Transport ECW-bodied Leyland Olympian ONTZ11/2R 735 (A735 YFS). It carried this Miller Homes design for some time.

Quite a low-key, but still noticeable, application for Edinburgh's then New Waverley Market appeared on Lothian Region Transport ECW Leyland Olympian ONTZ11/2R 731 (A731 YFS). The bus was pictured arriving at the Edinburgh Butterfly World.

Airline companies have utilised space on buses over the years too. Lothian Region Transport ECW-bodied Leyland Olympian ONTZ11/2R 669 (OFS 669Y) is seen in bright colours for Northwest Orient at Colinton in Edinburgh.

'Look no hands' – Lothian Region Transport ECW-bodied Leyland Olympian ONTZ11/2R 747 (B747 GSC) shows off its simple but effective livery for Hitachi as it approaches Clerwood terminus in Edinburgh.

Often advertisers split their campaign over a number of vehicles. Popular crisp manufacturer Walkers had flavour variations. ECW-bodied Leyland Olympian ONTZ11/2R 677 (OFS 677Y) is red, denoting the colour of ready salted flavour, at Torphin terminus, Edinburgh.

Lothian Region Transport Alexander RH-bodied Leyland Olympian 318 (E318 MSG), leaving Wallyford terminus, carried green livery for salt and vinegar flavoured Walkers Crisps. Other bus companies also had a pink variation for prawn cocktail flavour.

Seen high on Edinburgh's Calton Hill at a press photocall, this is Lothian Region Transport ECW-bodied Leyland Olympian ONTZ11/2R 752 (B752 GSC) for the AIDS campaign. The pink bus was supplemented by other buses with normal side ads for the Take Care campaign.

One of the most bizarre national campaigns was for a religious cause. Lothian Region Transport had two buses in the blue and yellow livery proclaiming 'Gouranga' and ECW-bodied Leyland Olympian ONTZ11/2R 754 (B754 GSC) is seen showing off the slogan in Princes Street, Edinburgh. The vehicles attracted curious looks during their time on the road.

Local advertising can generate a lot of interest. Lothian Region Transport Alexander RH-bodied Leyland Olympian 318 (E318 MSG) wore this livery for Portobello Beach in Edinburgh. This attraction had once been a very popular holiday destination but weather and cleanliness had led to a downturn in visitors. When photographed, the bus was at Muirhouse terminus.

Photographed at Moredun is Lothian Region Transport ECW-bodied Leyland Olympian ONTZ11/2R 790 (C790 SFS), which wore an advertising livery for the Thomson local phone directory – for many years an alternative to the Yellow Pages.

Showing a large car on the side of the vehicle, Lothian Region Transport ECW-bodied Leyland Olympian ONTZ11/2R 774 (C774 SFS) was used to promote Guy Salmon car rentals. It was captured near Tranent on its way into Edinburgh.

An extremely colourful advert aimed at the younger traveller was for Engie Benjy videos, seen here on Lothian Region Transport Alexander RH-bodied Leyland Olympian 344 (G344 CSG) as an offside vinyl. The bus is in Princes Street.

The same vehicle in the same location, Lothian Region Transport Alexander RH-bodied Leyland Olympian 344 (G344 CSG) later wore this offside vinyl advert for Tennent's beer and lager.

Occasionally an all-over advert can promote more than one product. In the case of Lothian Region Transport Alexander RH-bodied Leyland Olympian 313 (E313 MSG), it was one of two vehicles featuring an advert for Gulf petrol, which also proclaimed free gifts at Argos. Passengers helped create the 'live' appearance of the bus when their top halves appeared over the cartoon images painted on the side under the windows. The photo was taken at Newcraighall terminus.

Local Lothians radio station Radio Forth had two different adverts at the same time. Lothian Buses Alexander Royale-bodied Volvo Olympian 269 (P269 PSX) displays an olive green version at Ferniehill in Edinburgh.

Pictured at Seton Sands is Lothian Buses Alexander Royale-bodied Volvo Olympian 262 (P262 PSX), wearing a silver variant of advert for Forth FM 97.3.

Edinburgh local shop Carl Dyson, Sound and Vision Centre, made effective use of Lothian Region Transport ECW-bodied Leyland Olympian ONTZ11/2R 756 (B756 GSC) to promote its products. The bus is seen approaching Boswall Parkway in Edinburgh.

Another large shop to make use of all over advertising throughout the UK was Asda. Pictured here heading out of Edinburgh on the Old Dalkeith Road is Lothian Region Transport ECW-bodied Leyland Olympian ONTZ11/2R 762 (B762 GSC).

Controversial (and not very popular with passengers) contravision vinyls covered Lothian Buses Alexander Royale-bodied Volvo Olympians 272 and 284 (P272 PSX and P284 PSX) for Nokia mobile phones and the Carphone Warehouse. The fine dots used to cover the windows caused headaches and difficulty in seeing out. Both buses were on shuttle duty to Ingliston showground during the popular Royal Highland Show when pictured.

Part of another national campaign, Lothian Buses Alexander-bodied Volvo Olympian 969 (L969 WSC), seen in Princes Street in Edinburgh, disguised the passengers this time with its unusual livery for the Egg Money Mastercard.

Another example of a mega side advert is this vinyl for Scotland's favourite soft drink, Irn Bru, seen on Lothian Buses Wrightbus-bodied Volvo Gemini B7TL 769 (SN56 ACJ) in St Andrew Square, Edinburgh.

An eye-catching offside advert for Edinburgh's Telford College on Lothian Buses Wrightbus-bodied Volvo Gemini B7TL 723 (SN55 BMO) in St Andrew Square, Edinburgh.

A big national UK campaign was for Strongbow Cloudy Apple Cider. 762 (SN56 ABK), heading up the Mound in Edinburgh, was one of two Lothian Buses Wrightbus-bodied Volvo Gemini B7TLs to carry the advertising.

Lothian Buses Wrightbus-bodied Volvo Gemini B9TL 934 (SN09 CVV) wore this very striking orange livery for the Mammoths of the Ice Age exhibition at the National Museum of Scotland in Edinburgh in 2014. Again, the use of contravision over the windows was not popular with all its passengers. The bus was named *Murdo the Mammoth* and was photographed on the Mound.

The livery for McCain Oven Chips always looked rather half-finished. Again, it was a national UK-wide advert and in Edinburgh appeared on Lothian Buses Wrightbus-bodied Volvo Gemini B7TL 859 (SN57 DFO), seen in Princes Street.

Mobile phone technology is constantly changing and advertising on buses is now a regular sight. Lothian Buses Wrightbus-bodied Volvo Gemini B5TL 408 (BN64 CPV), seen approaching Haymarket, was one of a number that picked up grey vinyls for the Samsung Galaxy S8.

Lothian Buses Wrightbus-bodied Volvo Gemini B5TL 412 (BN64 CRF) carried this pink advert (including over the clear staircase panels) for Clinique beauty products and is seen at Sherrifhall Park & Ride site in Midlothian.

One of the biggest sellers now are PlayStation and Xbox games. Lothian Buses Wrightbus-bodied Volvo Gemini B5TL 416 (BN64 CRV) has wrap-around vinyls for PS4 *Call of Duty Black Ops* as it passes by Waverley Bridge in Edinburgh.

The BBC has started promoting both its TV and radio services on public transport. Lothian Buses Wrightbus-bodied Volvo Gemini B5TL 417 (BN64 CRX) is brightly adorned for BBC Sounds in this evening shot taken on Princes Street in Edinburgh.

Fresh out of its BBC advert contract, Lothian Buses Wrightbus-bodied Volvo Gemini B5TL 417 (BN64 CRX) was re-vinyled for the Royal Edinburgh Military Tattoo for 2019. The slogan 'Tradition with a Twist' is accompanied by a kaleidoscope view of the type of acts you can watch at the Tattoo on Edinburgh Castle Esplanade.

This bus attracted a lot of attention thanks to the fake tennis ball lodged in the rear window – so much so that the ball was removed. Lothian Buses Optare Solo 281, pictured at the West End terminus, displays an all-over livery for the Standard Life Group for contracted route 61, which employees can use between the two main headquarters in Edinburgh. Sadly, despite the support messages carried on the bus, Andy Murray was not to win Wimbledon that year.

During 2019, electric Lothian Buses Wrightbus Street Air 288 (SK67 FLG) picked up vinyls for Standard Life service 61 shortly after the Optare Solo was withdrawn. It is seen coming off Frederick Street after its short journey.

The use of buses to promote the annual Edinburgh Fringe and Edinburgh International Festival has become a regular occurrence. In 2014 Lothian Buses Wrightbus-bodied Volvo Gemini B9TL 918 (SN08 BYL) became all-over blue, including its wheels, and is seen near the Gyle.

Edinburgh Bus Tours open-top Wrightbus Eclipse Gemini 3-bodied Volvo B5TL 250 (ST66 LKP) was covered in pink vinyl in 2017 for the Edinburgh Fringe. It was on loan to East Coast Buses when photographed on a working of service 124 at Gullane.

Lothian Buses Volvo Gemini B5TL 413 (BN64 CRJ) dazzled passers-by at Ocean Terminal with its all-over yellow livery to promote the 2017 Edinburgh International Festival.

For the 2018 Edinburgh International Festival, Lothian Buses Volvo Gemini B5TL 415 (BN64 CRU), seen in Princes Street, became an almost identical yellow to the previous year on 413 but with different slogans.

First Glasgow Wrightbus Eclipse Gemini-bodied Volvo B9TL 37744 (SF09 LDV) with an eBay Christmas advert, awaiting departure from Silverburn bus station on the cross-city 57 service to Auchinairn. (Murdoch Currie)

Lothian Buses Wrightbus-bodied Volvo Gemini B9TL 906 (SN08 BXW) was one of two eBay advertisers the company operated. It is seen here arriving at the grounds of Riccarton University Campus.

The other vehicle, Lothian Buses Wrightbus-bodied Volvo Gemini B9TL 905 (SN08 BXV), shows the offside eBay ad as it turns at Ocean Terminal. The ad was unique to each operating area of the UK; the wording and Christmas tree were illuminated in the dark.

The eBay advert was to feature on the thousandth vinyled Wrightbus-bodied New Routemaster. London United LT169 (LTZ 1169), pictured near Covent Garden, had the honour of carrying it.

A growing trend across the country has been to support the various Pride events with specially decorated buses. The bus that started it all off was East London Wrightbus-bodied New Routemaster for London LT239 (LTZ 1239) in Ride with Pride colours. Corgi produced a scale model of it. (Andrew Chalmers)

Brighton & Hove Wrightbus Gemini-bodied Volvo B9TL 439 (BF12 KXS), named *Phil Starr*, is seen at Churchill Square, Brighton, in very colourful Pride colours. This bus has also been modelled by Corgi in the intricate livery. (Thomas McReynolds)

Oxford Pride was recognised by Oxford Bus Company Wrightbus Eclipse Gemini 2-bodied Volvo Hybrid 367 (V17 OXF). (Mark Lyons)

Lothian Buses Wrightbus Gemini 3-bodied hybrid Volvo B5TL 584 (SJ67 MGV) is seen on Edinburgh's Royal Mile, during the annual Pride Edinburgh March, in a very eye-catching merging rainbow colours livery.

Blockbuster movies feature heavily in bus advertising. To promote the James Bond film *Spectre*, East London Wrightbus-bodied New Routemaster for London LT359 (LTZ 1359) was given wrap-around vinyls. It was pictured about to cross over Oxford Street on the beginning of its journey on the 55. (Gordon Scott)

In other parts of the country, *Spectre* was given all-over offside ads. Lothian Buses Wrightbus-bodied Volvo Gemini B7TL 793 (SN56 AET) wore an example and is seen on Gilmerton Road, Edinburgh.

Spreading the word for Scottish Hydro Electric is Lothian Buses Plaxton Pointer-bodied Dennis Dart SLF 189 (Y189 CFS), turning onto Waverley Bridge, Edinburgh.

First Glasgow Wrightbus Eclipse Urban Volvo B7RLE 69066 (SF06 GYB) wore similar vinyls for Scottish Hydro Electric.

Lothian Buses Alexander Royale-bodied Volvo Olympian 252 (P252 PSX), turning into the roundabout at Cameron Toll shopping centre in Edinburgh, sports the double-decker version of the Scottish Hydro Electric advert.

First Wessex Alexander ALX400-bodied Volvo B7TL 32046 (W816 EOW) had the same advert but for Southern Electric.

First West Lothian Wrightbus Eclipse Gemini-bodied Volvo B9TL 37142 (SN57 HDC) was decorated in a special livery for the Homecoming Scotland 2009 event.

A number of London vehicles carried all-over advertising for Visa. Pictured in High Street, Stratford, First London Wrightbus Eclipse Gemini 2 Volvo B9TL VN36102 (BJ11 DSZ) was one. At the London 2012 Olympic Games, Visa was the exclusive payment services sponsor and the only card accepted at the Games. London 2012 represented Visa's most global and social activation since becoming an Olympic Games sponsor. There were around fifty vehicles prepared and they featured Usain Bolt on the side. Another Olympic sponsor, Samsung, also appeared on some buses. (Mark Lyons)

Eastern Scottish Alexander-bodied Leyland Olympian LL137 (A137 BSC) in a somewhat noticeable livery for Jockey shorts for men.

A rear view of First Glasgow Wrightbus Eclipse Gemini-bodied Volvo B9TL 37747 (SF09 LDZ) with a striking Sainsbury's/Argos/Tu advert in West Regent Street, Glasgow, on the cross-city 38 service from Newton Mearns to Easterhouse. (Murdoch Currie)

Heinz baked beans and Heinz tomato ketchup were widely advertised in Ireland and Northern Ireland for many years. Dublin Bus Alexander (Belfast)-bodied Volvo Olympian RV350 (97-D-350) shows off a half and half design for both.

A rear image of Dublin Bus Alexander (Belfast)-bodied Volvo Olympian RV350 (97-D-350) showing the mix of Heinz ads.

Dublin Bus Alexander (Belfast)-bodied Volvo Olympian RV413 (98-D-20413) was all blue for just Heinz baked beans.

Nearside of Dublin Bus Alexander (Belfast)-bodied Volvo Olympian RV350 (97-D-350) with the Heinz tomato ketchup ad prominently displayed.

Brighton & Hove Wrightbus Gemini 2-bodied Volvo B9TL 472 (BK13 OAU) used the famous snowman cartoon character to promote the Chestnut Tree House children's hospice care. (Andrew Chalmers)

Lothian Buses Wrightbus-bodied Volvo Gemini B7TL 769 (SN56 ACJ) also used the film *The Snowman* but this time to advertise Irn Bru, in keeping with the much-loved TV Christmas advert.

Pandas have proved popular on buses too. Tower Transit ADL-bodied Enviro400 DNH 39116 features the cuddly critters in an effort to entice people to visit Beautiful China.

Lothian Buses have had a tradition of applying different zoo animals and birds vinyls on buses that serve Edinburgh Zoo on route 26. Wrightbus-bodied Volvo Gemini B9TL 305 (SN09 CTX) ran as one of the zoo-themed fleet complete with pandas and Trek to China vinyls.

Lothian Buses Wrightbus-bodied Volvo Gemini B9TL 900 (SN08 BXO) received a special Edinburgh Zoo all-over ad for pandas Tian Tian ('Sweetie') and Yang Guang ('Sunshine') with the message 'Meet the Giants at Edinburgh Zoo'.

Stagecoach Western 50134 (511 OHU), named *Sweetie* after one of the pandas, was one of two Van Hool-bodied Astromega TD297 coaches that operated between Ayr and Edinburgh, offering the facility for passengers to disembark at Edinburgh Zoo to see the pandas and join the return journey later in the afternoon.

Alexander/Dennis Enviro400 Tower Transit DN33654 (SN11 BTO) had vinyls for the *Batman: Arkham Knight* PS4 game. PC games make big money and many are pre-ordered so advertising ahead of release is important.

London regularly promotes its world-famous and long-running musicals. London United Dennis Trident 2 TLA4 (SN53 EUK) in South Parade, Acton, with advertising for *The Phantom of the Opera*. (Mark Lyons)

Another example of a dedicated musical bus was London General Wrightbus Gemini-bodied Volvo B7TL WVL148 (LX53 AYZ) for *The Lion King*, seen at Victoria station.

Also at Victoria station was London General Wrightbus Gemini-bodied Volvo B7TL WVL150 (LX53 BJO) in all blue colours for *Mamma Mia*.

Connex Bus/Travel London Alexander-bodied Dennis Trident TA10 (V310 KGW) showing the offside treatment for musical *Chitty Chitty Bang Bang*. (Mark Lyons)

Showing the differences of the nearside, Connex Bus/Travel London TA10 (V310 KGW), the *Chitty Chitty Bang Bang* advertiser, sits near Oxford Street.

First London Plaxton President-bodied Dennis Trident TN959 (X959 HLT) is covered with
International Rescue vehicles to promote the remake live-action version of Gerry Anderson's
puppet show *Thunderbirds*.

Vinyl advertising can be complex or simple. London General Wrightbus-bodied New
Routemaster LT504 (LTZ 1504) heads towards Trafalgar Square with a fairly simple scheme for
Adidas's P.O.D. System trainers.

Basically in its normal red livery, London Central Wrightbus-bodied New Routemaster LT443 (LTZ 1443) advertises the PS4 *Spider-Man* game as it heads past Trafalgar Square.

A previous connection to the Marvel universe was Lothian Buses Wrightbus Gemini-bodied Volvo B9TL 853 (SN57 DFE) prior to the release of the movie *The Amazing Spider-Man*. It is seen turning into George Street during a diversion from Princes Street in Edinburgh.

Coca-Cola has had several large campaigns across London and these have utilised space on the NRMs. This night-time shot in Oxford Street shows London United Wrightbus-bodied New Routemaster LT152 (LTZ 1152) in the livery that was modelled by Corgi.

London United Wrightbus-bodied New Routemaster LT159 (LTZ 1159) shows the nearside Coca-Cola advert from the same campaign as it crosses Regent Street. Note the clever use of the Coca-Cola name on the mid panels.

There are ways that the same advert can be made to look different. London General Wrightbus-bodied New Routemaster LT483 (LTZ 1483) shows a mainly blue Nike Air 720 advert at Trafalgar Square.

Similarly liveried London United Wrightbus-bodied New Routemaster LT168 (LTZ 1168) has a red hue through its Nike Air 720 advert, also at Trafalgar Square.

A one-off and very memorable livery was applied to Metroline Wrightbus-bodied New Routemaster LT100 (LTZ 1100) for Fender Stratocaster. It's gone through a couple of design changes but is still in service in basically the same style. The photo was taken at Pimlico terminus.

The third version of the guitar livery that Metroline Wrightbus-bodied New Routemaster LT100 (LTZ 1100) has worn is for the Fender American Elite series. It is seen crossing Waterloo Bridge.

Metroline Plaxton President-bodied Volvo B7TL VP319 (LR52 BLV) took part in the Back the Bid London 2012 campaign. 'Back the Bid' buses were part of the largest public awareness campaign TfL has ever run. There were forty highly visible buses 'wrapped' in London 2012 branding that demonstrated TfL and the Mayor's total commitment to bringing the Olympic Games to London in 2012. (Mark Lyons)

In the same theme, Lothian Buses Wrightbus Gemini-bodied Volvo B9TL 382 (SN11 EDJ) is seen at Restalrig in a very attractive livery for Go Edinburgh Back the Bid 2016.

Sports shoes and accessories are also popular with bus advertising space. London United Wrightbus-bodied New Routemaster LT145 (LTZ 1145) reaches Parliament Square in Nike React livery.

At Trafalgar Square, Abellio Wrightbus-bodied New Routemaster LT605 (LTZ 1165) carries vinyls for the Vans brand.

All sorts of products and services feature in all-over bus advertising. East London Wrightbus-bodied New Routemaster LT408 (LTZ 1408) carries an advert for TalkTalk Broadband.

Unlike the hand-painted all-over ads of the past, vinyl wraps tend to be applied for a matter of weeks. Blink and you can miss some. London General Wrightbus-bodied New Routemaster LT504 (LTZ 1504) sports vinyls for the Sony Xperia XZ3 smartphone.

Fashion designers find buses a great way to advertise. London Central Wrightbus-bodied New Routemaster LT434 (LTZ 1434) is dwarfed by the London Eye with a design for Mango.

Two-tone green stripes appear on London Central Wrightbus-bodied New Routemaster LT429 (LTZ 1429) for another fashion company, Jo Malone.

An advert with an enticement to buy the product. East London Central Wrightbus-bodied New Routemaster LT271 (LTZ 1271) gives details of a Danone Actimel breakfast competition.

Undoubtedly one of my favourite of the NRM advertisers was displayed on London General Wrightbus-bodied New Routemaster LT68 (LTZ 1068) seen at Victoria. With its film strip use of the passenger windows, this L'Oreal Paris Studio Pro wrap got a lot of attention from passers-by.

Very pink and very spottable at King's Cross was London United Wrightbus-bodied New Routemaster LT159 (LTZ 1159) advertising Lastminute.com.

A specific campaign for Christmas 2018 is seen on London General Wrightbus-bodied New Routemaster LT478 (LTZ 1478), approaching Westminster promoting Schweppes Merry Mixes.

New Routemaster LT4 (LTZ 1004) was one of a number that appeared in a very bright green livery to promote Uber Eats. It was pictured at night heading through the neon lights of Piccadilly Circus.

Some all-over vinyls need fairly close inspection to understand what the adverts are actually for. One such example is Arriva London North Wrightbus-bodied New Routemaster LT4 (LTZ 1004) at Victoria, vinyled for HSBC UK Connected Money.

At first look, Arriva London South Wrightbus-bodied New Routemaster LT718 (LTZ 1718) near Waterloo station appears to be advertising Yahoo, but on closer inspection it is actually for American Express.

Magnum comes up with some very distinctive adverts for their ice creams. Photographed at Marble Arch, Arriva London South Wrightbus-bodied New Routemaster LT345 (LTZ 1345) was split pink on one side and grey on the other for a Magnum campaign. The advert was also applied in reverse on other NRMs.

London Central Wrightbus-bodied New Routemaster LT422 (LTZ 1422) turns around Trafalgar Square showing one of the many Michael Kors wraps that have been worn. There have also been a number of different styles over the years.

Arriva London South Wrightbus-bodied New Routemaster LT338 (LTZ 1338) advertised Flora Original spread – quite an unusual product to feature in all-over advertising. It was photographed in Oxford Street.

Cadbury's have run campaigns for many of their popular brands of chocolate. London United Wrightbus-bodied New Routemaster LT120 (LTZ 1120) was one of a number to advertise Cadbury Crunchie and is seen at Victoria.

London Central Wrightbus-bodied New Routemaster LT456 (LTZ 1456) carried a distinctive white-based livery for Pizza Express and its Hawaiian variety. It was caught at Portland Place.

London United Alexander Dennis Enviro400 ADH45008 (SN60 BYC) can be spotted at a distance with its busy vinyls for Jelly Belly beans.

Colourful vinyls on Abellio Wrightbus-bodied New Routemaster LT612 (LTZ 1612) for Swatch watches are seen passing through Westminster.

For a good few months over 2018 and 2019, brightly coloured yellow NRMs appeared including London United Wrightbus-bodied New Routemaster LT161 (LTZ 1161) with different designs for Chiquita bananas. It is arriving at King's Cross.

London General Wrightbus-bodied New Routemaster LT274 (LTZ 1274), with similar slogans for Chiquita bananas, is seen crossing the River Thames.

Another photograph of London United Wrightbus-bodied New Routemaster LT161 (LTZ 1161), one of the Chiquita bananas buses, turning into Caledonian Road.

The yellow colours mean that Chiquita bananas London United Wrightbus-bodied New Routemaster LT161 (LTZ 1161) can be easily seen in all weather conditions.

London Go Ahead Wrightbus 2 Hybrid-bodied Volvo B5LH WHV 115 (BV66 VHR) was one of a few promoting the benefits of an Innocent breakfast near Kensington.

Tower Transit Alexander Dennis-bodied Enviro400 DNH 39113 (SN12 ARF) was another advertiser for an airline – in this case Air India.

Charities benefit from the widespread advertising they can get from wrapping a bus fully or partially. London Metroline Wrightbus Gemini-bodied Volvo hybrid VW1199 (LK62 DVJ) was photographed waiting time at Victoria station, displaying details of the Children with Cancer fundraiser.

A very yellow advert with quite an amount of reading in it appeared on Tower Transit Wrightbus Gemini-bodied Volvo hybrid VN36113 (BJ11 DVP) for the London Metropolitan University, seen off of Oxford Street.

New in Edinburgh and Glasgow, for 2019, was the Bustaurant dining and tour experience, using a beautifully refurbished ADL Plaxton President-bodied Dennis Trident – formerly Lothian Buses 594 (X594 USC). Rather than apply wrapped vinyl on the bus, the stunning Scottish images were hand painted in the traditional way by local Glasgow graffiti artist Rogue One.

Former Stagecoach Busways/Western Alexander-bodied Volvo Olympian 16726 (N726 LTN) became a mobile classroom for the Royal Zoological Society of Scotland. It was pictured in Princes Street in Edinburgh.

J. J. Kavanagh & Sons Setra S416GT-HD 09-KE-1 in central Dublin advertising Supermac's Burgers. (Alistair Train)

Passing through Musselburgh in East Lothian is Eastern Scottish Alexander Leyland Olympian ONLXB/1R LL124 (ALS 124Y), featuring the distinctive colours and logo of McDonald's restaurants.

Tally Ho! Alexander Dennis-bodied Enviro200 DK61 GXY is seen in Kingsbridge with an attractive design for local holiday cottage specialist company Toad Hall Cottages. (Alistair Train)

Plymouth Citybus have a heritage bus decked out in vinyls with black and white photographs depicting many notable events in Plymouth's history. The vehicle is Alexander Dennis-bodied Enviro400 508 (WF63 LYS), which was photographed on Royal Parade in Plymouth. (Alistair Train)

Translink Belfast Metro Wrightbus Gemini-bodied Volvo 2213 (SEZ 2213) was photographed in the centre of Belfast with a cartoon-style advert for a Phoenix Natural Gas campaign. This complimented a series of eye-catching and humorous posters that appeared in the eastern part of Northern Ireland. (Alistair Train)

Stagecoach Devon were involved in a tourist initiative in 2011 when they operated the North Devon Surf & Cycle bus. Northern Counties Palatine-bodied 16017 (P817 GMU) was captured entering Barnstaple bus station. The bus was able to take surfboards and bicycles on board. The service managed a couple of seasons before the funding collapsed. East London operated a similar vehicle. (Alistair Train)

Perryman's Optare Solo 028 (MX07 NTU) leaving Golden Square, Berwick upon Tweed, advertising Marshall's outdoor clearance superstore. The bus transferred later to Borders Buses. (Alistair Train)

Stagecoach North Scotland Plaxton Profile-bodied Volvo B7R 53334 (448 GWL, ex-SV09 EFZ) is in High Street, Banchory, on the 201 Braemar–Aberdeen service. The Spotty Bag Shop is a family-run discount store in Banff, Aberdeenshire. (Murdoch Currie)

All red for HB ice cream, promoting a 'Random Acts of Happiness' campaign, Dublin Bus Alexander Dennis ALX400-bodied Volvo B7TL AV397 (04-D-20397) passes through the centre of Dublin. (Alistair Train)

Dublin Buses ADL Enviro 400 EV100 (08-D-30100) heads into Dublin centre with vinyls for Carroll's of Tullamore New York Deli.

Go South Coast ADL-bodied Enviro400 MMC 1634 (HF66 CFA) was photographed in Gervis Road in Bournemouth wearing a particularly colourful livery for the AUB (Arts University Bournemouth). (Tommy McReynolds)

Brighton & Hove Mercedes Benz Citaro 2 artic 109 (BD57 WDM) in Old Steine, Brighton. The vehicle is branded in bright geometric colours as the 'Happies not Hippies' bus in celebration of the South Coast resort's bohemian lifestyle and was inspired by a campaign in Chile that sought to make people think before stereotyping others. (Tommy McReynolds)

Kellogs Rice Krispies Squares was a colourful national campaign seen across the country. One example was First Devon and Cornwall Plaxton President-bodied Dennis Trident 33177 (LR02 LYW), seen on Torquay Strand. (Alistair Train)

The use of all-over advertising to promote travelling by bus has taken many forms over the years. Brighton & Hove Wrightbus Gemini 2-bodied Volvo B9TL 490 (BJ63 UJU), named *Herbert Toms*, was photographed at Old Steine, Brighton, wearing a livery encouraging people to 'Get on. Go Somewhere'. (Tommy McReynolds)

In similar vein, with messages to 'Get Fitter' and 'Hop on and Hop off' along the route, Brighton & Hove Wrightbus Gemini 2-bodied Volvo B9TL 420 (BJ11 XHW), named *Dr Richard Russell*, was photographed at the Old Steine, Brighton, end of the route. (Tommy McReynolds)

All-over adverts can have a serious message to spread. First Aberdeen Wright Renown-bodied Volvo B10BLE 62166 (Y631 RSA) was photographed in Union Street in Clan Cancer Support vinyls. This local charity, based in Aberdeen, provides emotional and practical support to people affected by cancer, their family, carers and friends.

GG CT Plus 220 (77056) is an ADL Caetano Nimbus-bodied Dart 8.8 SLF captured on North Parade, Guernsey. It is decked out as a mobile directory for local businesses. Some of these buses transferred to companies on the mainland, including First West Lothian, in 2018. (Tommy McReynolds)

First Glasgow Wrightbus Gemini-bodied Volvo B7TL 32569 (SF54 OTL) displays a powerful vinyl-based advert for the film *Terminator Salvation*. This type of advert certainly attracts attention, although most tend to be on the dark side.

Golden Tours MCV DD103-bodied Volvo B9TL 106 (BF62 UYP) is one of a number that have carried all-over publicity for a shuttle between central Edinburgh and the Harry Potter Studio Tour near Watford. It is seen approaching Victoria.

The Harry Potter Studio London attraction has also been advertised in Dublin. J. J. Kavanagh & Sons East Lancs-bodied Myllennium Vyking 02-W-7035 is seen in service in Waterford in all-over vinyls wrap. (Alistair Train)

Clydeside Alexander AV-bodied Volvo Ailsa Mark 2 B55-10 J895 (KSD 95W) was one of two all-over advertising vehicles for Food Giant – a now defunct UK supermarket chain owned by also defunct Somerfield. (Donald MacRae)

First York Wright Gemini-bodied Volvo B9TL 37069 (YK57 EZZ) carries an all-over pink advertisement for contactless payments – a new way of paying your bus fare which is rapidly becoming the most popular form of payment on public transport.

Reading Buses ADL-bodied Enviro400 1212 (DU61 FVY), seen departing from Victoria Coach Station, displays information about the Vamooz app-based crowdfunding travel scheme. Using the app, customers can suggest a destination of their choice for a day trip across the North. Vamooz rewards people encouraging others to travel by lowering the price for everyone.

The Original London Sightseeing Tour Optare Visionaire-bodied Volvo B9TL VXE 725 (YJ11 TVF) negotiates a tight corner at Victoria advertising Guatemala as a holiday destination.

Pictured in Union Street in Aberdeen, First Aberdeen ADL-bodied Enviro300 67802 (SN13 COH) promotes the local council initiative Shaping Aberdeen.

First Wessex National Roe-bodied Leyland Olympian 9542 (NTC 141Y) in a bright and cheerful livery for Littlesea Luxury Holiday Homes. (Mark Lyons)

First Edinburgh Wrightbus Gemini-bodied Volvo B9TL 37137 (SN57 HCV) hurls along Princes Street with a summery Irn Bru all-over advert. Irn Bru has had a number of campaigns over the years.

Translink Metro Wrightbus Gemini-bodied Volvo B9TL 2334 (SEZ 2334) was pictured in Belfast in Coors Light vinyls. (Gordon Scott)

Stagecoach Plaxton Panther-bodied Volvo B13RT 54125 (SP62 CKF) was originally new to Rennie's of Dunfermline. For a while it carried this bright livery for Scotland's Charity Air Ambulance Charity and was seen in the West End of Edinburgh.

Cardiff Bus East Lancs Darwen Olympus-bodied Scania N270D 472 (CN57 FGD), arriving in Westgate Street in Cardiff, displays an all-over advert for sports events around Cardiff and Wales. (Andrew Chalmers)

Bus Eireann Expressway Scania Irizar SE 33 (15-D-2637) exits Dublin coach station adorned in various multi-coloured diagonal stripes and lines but no advertising of any description. It certainly stands out in the traffic.

Bus Eireann Expressways Scania Irizar SE 33 (15-D-6215), departing from Dublin coach station with somewhat animated passengers, advertises Brown Bag Films, one of the world's most exciting, original and successful creative-led animation studios, founded in Dublin.

Sporting a very dramatic all-over advert, this is Bus Eireann Wrightbus Gemini 3-bodied Volvo B5TL VWD 22 (151-D-19010) celebrating the Women of the Rising in 1916.

New to Lothian Region Transport as their 765 (B765 GSC), this ECW-bodied Leyland Olympian was sold to Dodd's of Troon and re-registered as B7 CCE. After conversion into a partial open-topper, it carried out a number of promotional tours for the *Scottish Sun* newspaper. The photo was taken in the Tesco Musselburgh car park.

Reading Buses ADL-bodied Enviro 400 209 (SN11 BTF) is a regular performer on Greenline services 702 to central London and 703 to Heathrow Terminal 5. It is seen on the 703, heading for Bracknell, at the Parish Church stop in Windsor with all-over advertising for Reading Football Club. (Andrew Chalmers)

Stagecoach South ADL Enviro400 19063 (MX56 FSP) is at Hard Bus & Coach Interchange with eye-catching vinyls for Portsmouth Historic Dockyards, which offers a range of events and seasonal festivals for every adventurer. (Andrew Chalmers)

Go Ahead North East 5419 (NK15 EOL) is a DF/Wright-bodied Streetlite Max Micro-Hybrid wearing advertising for Beamish – the living museum of the North.

Stagecoach Western Plaxton Panther-bodied Volvo B13RT 54128 (YX63 NFT) promoting the Young Scot Awards 2018 at the Buchanan bus station in Glasgow.

EGZ 4848 is a Jonckheere B11R-bodied Volvo B9R of Hannon Coaches, who operate from Glasgow to Belfast, (new as LSK 555 with Parks of Hamilton) in all-over advertising for ice hockey team Belfast Giants (as official coach partner) and the team's main sponsor Stena Line Ferries.

Vinyls work well on tour buses too. Seen on Johnston Terrace is Wrightbus Eclipse Gemini 3-bodied Volvo B5TL 249 (ST66 LKO), wearing a stunning wrap-round vinyl that is used on the various open-top routes of Edinburgh Bus Tours – part of the Lothian Buses group. It was originally displayed at the 2016 Euro Bus Expo in Birmingham.

First Pioneer East Lancs-bodied Dennis Arrow 31952 (S452 SLL) advertising a short-lived radio station broadcast by Southampton Football Club. The Saint regularly featured current players presenting their own shows. (Mark Lyons)

Yellow Buses Alexander-bodied Volvo Citybus 207 (E207 GCG), rather oddly advertising a competing mode of transport – United Taxis – was pictured in Bridge Street, Christchurch. (Mark Lyons)

Eastern Scottish ECW-bodied Leyland Olympian LL107 (ULS 107X) in painted all-over advertising for the Woolco branch in Livingston, West Lothian. This was part of the Woolworths empire, all sadly now gone.

Seen in Dublin, Bus Eireann Expressway Scania K400 Irizar i6 SE20 (12-D-13477) has worn a number of different liveries in its lifetime. The vinyls here promote *Macalla 1916* – a suite of music with song and narration reflecting on the events of Easter 1916, which played a pivotal role in the birth of a nation.

Bus Eireann Wrightbus VWD41 (151-C-7156) in central Cork, carrying a wrap for radio station Today FM. (Alistair Train)

Stagecoach Highland Alexander Dennis-bodied Enviro200 36953 (YC63 LGZ) has a livery split down the middle. The nearside promotes Citylink Gold services linking Inverness to Glasgow. It is seen approaching the centre of Inverness.

The other side of Stagecoach Highland Alexander Dennis-bodied Enviro200 36953 (YC63 LGZ) with blue base advert for Megabus.com services to Glasgow, Edinburgh and Perth from Inverness.

Other parts of the group have had similar advertising. Stagecoach East Scotland ADL-bodied Enviro300 27603 (SP59 CTF) sits at Dunfermline bus station with nearside adverts for the Citylink 900 service between Edinburgh and Glasgow.

Eastern Scottish Alexander-bodied Leyland Olympian LL117 (ALS 117Y) descends Castle Street in Edinburgh with an all-over painted advert for a local firm, The Carpet Mill.

There have been some very unusual products demanding all-over adverts. Eastern Scottish ECW-bodied Leyland Olympian ONLXB/1R LL113 (ULS 113X) leaves Edinburgh bus station covered in giant Tipp-Ex correction fluid containers.

Tartan-clad buses have been popular in Scotland. Some years ago, Eastern Scottish LL129 (ALS 129Y), photographed at Picardy Place in Edinburgh, appeared in this very intricate livery for Stewarts Cream of the Barley – a classic blended Scotch whisky with a history that reaches far back into the 1800s.

First Borders Wrightbus-bodied Volvo B9TL 37133 (SN57 HDH) was one of a number of vehicles that picked up purple tartan vinyls promoting service X62, now operated by Borders Buses of the West Coast Motors group. The photo was taken in Waterloo Place at the start of its long journey to Peebles.

Lothian Buses Wrightbus Gemini-bodied Volvo B9TL 856 (SN57 DFJ) wears a green tartan for Macmillan Cancer Support and was named, through an online poll of customers, *Hamish*. The bus has worked on city routes and has also been loaned to Lothian Country and East Coast Buses, appearing in deepest Midlothian, West Lothian and East Lothian, where it was photographed at Strawberry Corner near Wallyford.

Seen departing from the Transport Interchange in Galashiels, former demonstrator Scania N280UD ADL Enviro MMC 11622 (YN16 CFU), now with Borders Buses, is in the distinctive tartan vinyl wrap-round for the My Name's Doddie Foundation motor neuron disease fund-raising campaign. Dodie Weir OBE is one of rugby's most recognisable personalities, having earned sixty-one caps for Scotland during his career.

Heart Radio covers large parts of the country and has used the media of buses to advertise its frequencies. London General Wrightbus-bodied New Routemaster LT482 (LTZ 1482) shows a recent campaign as it heads away from Trafalgar Square.

Pictured in Hinton Road, Bournemouth, this is Wilts & Dorset East Lancs-bodied Myllennium Vyking 1825 (HF05 GGE) with its vinyls for Heart Radio. (Mark Lyons)

At St Andrews Cross roundabout in Plymouth is Plymouth City Bus ADL Enviro400 304 (WF63 LZD), also featuring Heart Radio vinyls. (Andrew Chalmers)

Reading Buses 706 (YP67 XCA) in Heart Radio promoting vinyls. 706 is the only example of Reading's seventeen E400 city-bodied Scania bio-gas buses not to carry purple route branding (although it was delivered in this scheme). Its front end carries the undertaking's silver generic scheme. (Mark Lyons)

Lothian Buses Wrightbus-bodied Volvo B5LH 551 (SA15 VUB), which has spent a significant amount of its life in a white-based livery. During 2017 and 2018 it carried two variations of Poppy Scotland messages for Remembrance Day. The 2018 version remained on the bus until late May 2019, when it became all white again. This shot was taken near the end of its Poppy days and while on loan to Lothian Country Buses, heading to Bathgate in West Lothian.

Various Poppy campaigns are held throughout the UK. Plymouth City Bus ADL-bodied Enviro400 521 (WJ65 BYM) wears a scheme on Royal Parade in Plymouth. (Andrew Chalmers)

The Poppy bus campaign started principally in London. London Central Wrightbus-bodied New Routemaster LT429 (LTZ 1429) shows off one of the styles that have featured. (Gordon Scott)

London Stagecoach 15152 (LX59 COU) Poppy Bus. 2012 was the first year that TfL wrapped buses for Remembrance Day and only two vehicles were treated (both with Stagecoach). By 2018 Abellio, Go-Ahead London, Arriva, Stagecoach, Metroline, Tower Transit and RATP supported TfL's activity by funding the poppy wrapping of several buses. (Mark Lyons)

Oxford Bus Company Plaxton Panther-bodied Volvo B12B 52 (BB07 OXF) is seen in High Street, Oxford, en route to Victoria, advertising the Oxford Creation Theatre, whose shows aren't centred in actual theatres but taken to castles, antique mirror tents, college gardens, bookshops, factories or wherever the stories take them. (Mark Lyons)

Plymouth City Bus Plaxton President Dennis Trident 426 (Y808 TGH) in Derry's Cross with a colourful advert display for Larry Speare Carpets. (Mark Lyons)

During 2019, Lothian Buses celebrated 100 years and out-shopped newly delivered Alexander Dennis Enviro400 XLB-bodied Volvo B8L 1125 (SJ19 OZD) in a special livery, recognising some of the rich history of the company and its predecessors in Edinburgh. The bus is seen beside the famous Hunter's Tryst pub at Oxgangs.

Another picture of centenary-liveried Lothian Buses Alexander Dennis Enviro400 XLB-bodied Volvo B8L 1125 (SJ19 OZD) at Cameron Toll, on a diversion to service 31.

Lothian Region Transport Alexander-bodied Leyland Atlantean AN68/1R 664 (GSC 664X) was one of the black and white single-door batch used for city tours and on the airport service 100. For a while it ran in all gold to promote the Gold of the Pharaohs exhibition in Edinburgh and is seen on the approach to Edinburgh Airport.

A slightly different use for an all-over advert. Ensignbus Wrightbus Gemini-bodied Volvo B7TL 392 MBF (new to London General), converted to an open-topper, received a very topical all-over contract during 2018 for the Brexit – Leave Means Leave campaign. It spent much of its time driving without passengers around central London.